A Hand for Spelling

A spelling scheme in joined writing

BOOK 4a

By Charles Cripps

A Hand for Spelling Book 4a
LL 01627
ISBN 1 85503 212 0

First published 1988
New edition 1995
Reprinted 1997, 1998, 2000, 2003

LDA, Duke Street, Wisbech, Cambs, PE13 2AE
3195 Wilson Dr, NW, Grand Rapids, MI 49544, USA

Contact our customer services department to find out more about the complete *A Hand For Spelling* range. Tel: 01945 463441 Fax: 01945 587361

The Author

Charles Cripps was formerly a tutor at the University of Cambridge Institute of Education. The focus of his work is on communication skills for children with learning difficulties.

He lectures nationally and internationally on the teaching of spelling and handwriting and has contributed to the National Curriculum proposals. He has many publications including: *Spelling through the Literacy Hour, LDA,* and a software publication for the teaching of spelling.

This revised edition of *A Hand for Spelling* is the result of ongoing classroom investigation regarding the link between the teaching of joined writing and the catching of spelling.

Charles Cripps would also like to acknowledge the valuable contribution to the revised edition by Janet Ede. Many of the spelling activities are based on, or have been taken directly from, the original Activity Books in which Janet Ede was the co-author.

Charles Cripps is also grateful to Robin Cox for his advice on the content of the programme and to Jo Finch for the idea of letter formation snakes in Book 1a.

Introduction

The National Curriculum has presented schools with a new agenda for the teaching of handwriting. At all Key Stages the importance of well-formed legible handwriting is emphasised. There has also been a gradual acceptance of the value of children beginning joined writing from a much earlier age. It is no longer the sole responsibility of teachers in the junior years. The new proposals now require children to produce handwriting which is joined and legible at Level 3 in Key Stage 1.

The requirements of the National Curriculum are totally endorsed and supported within *A Hand for Spelling*. The rationale behind this programme also argues that the Level Descriptions as outlined in the National Curriculum can best be met when teachers recognise the value of introducing children to joined writing from the beginning. This programme is based on the strong principle that the free physical movement through the word contributes to success in spelling.

Revised Edition

This revised edition is the result of ongoing investigation in the classroom into the teaching of spelling and joined writing. It offers the following features:

▷ Each letter pattern is introduced with a section concentrating on handwriting where letters are produced in a connected form. This is followed by work on the spelling of words with that pattern. Activities providing practice and consolidation follow on directly from each letter pattern.

▷ A new section on p.viii sets out the rationale behind the teaching of joined writing and spelling and gives suggestions on good practice. Pages x-xi give guidelines on how to use the worksheets and how to select worksheets appropriately to meet the needs of an individual pupil.

▷ A complete contents list for the whole scheme enables you to pinpoint letter patterns required to meet the needs of groups or individual pupils.

▷ Finally, because *A Hand for Spelling* is a spelling scheme in joined writing, it leaves you free to adopt any handwriting style, as might have been agreed in the school policy. However, this new edition does provide an improved model which offers a clear, consistent demonstration of movement through letters and the joins between letters.

Contents

A Hand for Spelling has been designed as a spelling scheme in joined writing and provides you with material to cover the teaching of spelling and handwriting as outlined in the National Curriculum.

Books 1a and 1b introduce children to a range of pre-writing activities to promote pencil control and correct letter formation.

A Hand For Spelling Phonetic Stage introduces children, who are at the phonetic stage of spelling, to write words which contain the same letter pattern and the same sound unit. This is an important developmental stage which children reach and requires practice before passing through to the transitional stage and onto standard or correct spelling.

Books 2a to 4b provide children with the opportunity of writing letter patterns and then looking at words containing the same letter pattern irrespective of their sound. All the words used in this programme are a careful selection based on the words used by 5-11 year-old children in their writing.

A Hand for Spelling Book 1a

Book 1a gives children practice in pencil control and fine motor movements. Scribbles and patterns will also help develop pencil control, visual perception and hand-eye co-ordination. It is important that these are practised in art media as well as with the pencil or crayon. The final worksheets in Book 1a help children learn to recognise and write the individual letters. It is at this stage that they must also begin to learn correct letter formation and the names of the letters.

A Hand for Spelling Book 1b

Book 1b supports and helps to cement the skills introduced in Book 1a. Pencil control and correct letter formation are essential prerequisites before moving on to Book 2a or the Phonetic Stage book. When practising the letters the children should continue using the names of the letters.

A Hand for Spelling Books – Phonetic Stage, 2a and 2b

These books are based on words used by children aged 5-7

Phonetic Stage

The Phonteic Stage provides practice, within the phonetic stage of spelling, of writing words which contain the same spelling pattern and the same sound. Although children are writing down what they <u>hear</u> it is also important to begin promoting the visual aspect of spelling, that is, encourage the children to write down what they <u>see</u>. Therefore, when practising these letter patterns the children should continue to use the letter names. The words in this book contain the five short vowel sounds. With the exception of the 'ch', 'sh', 'th', 'qu' beginnings and the 'ck', 'll', 'ss' endings, all words begin and end with single consonants only.

A Hand For Spelling Books 3a and 3b

These books are based on words used by children aged 7-9.

A Hand for Spelling Books 4a and 4b

These books are based on words used by children aged 9-11.

The Teaching of Handwriting

The National Curriculum emphasises the importance of handwriting by stating that by the end of Key Stage 1, children should have developed a comfortable handwriting style which is joined and legible.

The inference taken from this statement is that children should be introduced as early as possible to the making of letters through patterns. Pre-school children do a great deal of scribbling and inventive writing. They should be encouraged at this stage, and in the reception class, to discover letter shapes and movements in these forms. The shapes and movements should then be developed into making letters in connected form.

The teaching of joined writing from as early as possible has many advantages:

▷ It is no longer necessary to make the change from print to joined writing at Levels 2 and 3.

▷ From the beginning it will be clear to children that words are separate. This helps children to acquire the concept of a 'word' from the very early stages of writing.

▷ Correct letter formation is encouraged from the beginning since the ligatures lead naturally into the correct starting point for each letter.

▷ Joined writing helps children to develop a legible style that exhibits 'regularity of size and shape of letters' (a requirement of Key Stage 1).

▷ Good spelling is encouraged because letter patterns are necessarily connected when writing a word.

COMMON CONCERNS

The following concerns are commonly raised by teachers.

Are children able to read joined writing and will it present any problems in early reading?

The only practical implication is that children should have a chance to read both print and joined writing. The sensible level of discussion with children who are beginning to read will support the need to spot the differences and to talk about letters, joins and whole words. Certainly joined writing should be used when writing in a child's book although both joined writing and print script may be used in displays around the school and classroom. Words which are for reading only are likely to be in print and words that are likely to be written should be in joined writing. In other words there is a style for reading and a style for writing. Experience has shown, however, that children are able to read both.

How should capital letters be taught?

Capital letters are printed and it is not necessary to join them to the lower case letter.

Won't the early teaching of joined writing affect legibility?

In any handwriting programme, the first priority should be legibility. If handwriting is the means of communication then it must be easy to read with letters properly formed. At a later stage, children will require different levels of writing for different purposes, namely a very fast hand for personal notes; a clear but quick hand for general use and finally a formal hand for special occasions. The second priority is speed, because speed of writing has been shown to influence spelling. In most cases the fast printer is not as fast as the writer who uses a cursive style.

Does it matter what handwriting style we use with A Hand for Spelling?

No. *A Hand for Spelling* leaves children free to use any style of handwriting. However, in line with National Curriculum recommendations, children must be encouraged to develop a personal style by breaking away from the taught model. This will only be successful if the foundations are secure. The personal hand usually begins to take shape towards the end of the primary years and is an indication of the writer's confidence and maturity.

TEACHING POINTS

In delivering a handwriting programme, attention should also be given to the following:

▷ Allow plenty of practice of pre-writing skills involving scribbling and pattern work which will help develop perception and hand-eye co-ordination. This can also link in with art and craft work.

▷ Observe how children form their letters at all stages and be careful not to be influenced by the look or appearance of the finished product, if done unobserved.

▷ The teaching of print should not be neglected and can be introduced as art work. At the beginning of Key Stage 2 children should be taught to develop 'legible handwriting in both joined up and printed styles'.

▷ Give specific attention to pencil control, pencil grip and posture, being alert to the different needs of left-handed children. (Assorted pencil grips are available from LDA.)

LEFT-HANDED CHILDREN

Provision must be made for left-handed children. If these children are taught *how to be left-handed* then they can write as freely and legibly as right-handed children. The following practical considerations all help.

▷ Left-handers should always sit on the left-hand side of a right-hander. This will avoid their arms colliding.

▷ The left-hander needs to have the paper on the left hand side of the mid line of the body. After tilting the paper to a comfortable angle it should be pushed about five centimetres away from the body. Incorrect paper position will usually result in an awkward, twisted grip. Some left-handers may need to hold the pencil a little further away from the point than right-handers so that the writing is not obscured by the thumb knuckle.

▷ Ideally, left-handers should have the light coming over the left shoulder.

▷ It is also important for left-handers to sit on a higher chair. This position, together with the paper being pushed away from the body, will prevent the elbow locking into the side of the body when the writing has reached only half way across the page.

▷ In A Hand for Spelling the design of some activities which demand writing from memory are more suitable for right-handed children. The teacher may therefore wish to make a model more suitable for left-handed children by cutting and pasting the appropriate pages before photocopying.

The Teaching of Spelling

It has been shown that good handwriting and spelling go together: the work of Cripps and Cox (1989) indicates that where the two skills are taught together, children do become more confident in looking at and writing words. They are more willing to 'have a go' and are certainly more able to look critically at their work and identify misspellings. It is therefore logical and more economic to link the teaching of spelling to the teaching of handwriting.

In order to promote spelling through handwriting it is important that children practise patterns or strings of letters which belong to the English writing system. This means that if, for example, children are rehearsing 'ood', then they would be encouraged to use this pattern in words such as 'good', 'wood', and 'food'. The most significant difference in this word group compared with the lists of words traditionally used for spelling is that they are grouped according to *visual structure*. This is because it is primarily by *looking* that we remember spelling. If we are uncertain about how to write a word then we write it down to see if it looks right. The decision about correctness can be made when the word is seen written down.

In the early stages of writing development it is true that children do rely on what they hear. They write 'wot' for 'what', because the word sounds like 'pot', 'hot', 'not', etc. They also write 'sed' for' 'said' and 'thay' for 'they'. This is the phonetic stage of spelling and it is for this reason that the words in the Phonetic Stage book are grouped according to sound and visual appearance only. However, if children are to become confident spellers we must help them to cultivate visual skills. In other words, they must always be encouraged to look at the whole word and try to write down what they *see* rather than what they *hear*.

You can also promote the catching of spelling by helping children to look for words within words. Children can begin to look for common letter patterns by starting with those that occur in their own names. During any discussion with children about the look of a word you should always use the letter names rather than the sounds, because it is the names that provide the only reliable and consistent way of describing the spelling of a word.

It is important that children learn to write words 'from memory'. This can be done by encouraging children to look closely at a word before writing it. You can point out the interesting features and challenge the child to reproduce the word without copying. It is here that handwriting becomes so important because 'speed of writing is clearly basic to spelling progress' (Peters, 1985) and speed is determined by legibility and letter formation. Where writing from memory is continually encouraged, the qualitative level of spelling is much higher.

Obviously teachers must be careful that children do not become so concerned about the secretarial skills of spelling and handwriting that the essential composing aspects are lost. Spelling and handwriting serve writing and their prime function is to convey legibly the writer's message to the reader.

The teacher who maintains a careful balance between compositional skills on the one hand and the importance of word inspection and writing the different word structures on the other, will find that children's confidence and pleasure in writing will increase.

Using A Hand for Spelling

STRUCTURE OF THE SCHEME

A Hand for Spelling consists of nine books of photocopy masters designed for 5-11 year-olds and older pupils with learning difficulties.

The first stage follows on from the natural, free scribble movements which children make when they first hold a pencil. These are then harnessed into pattern work from which a running hand will follow. Books 1a and 1b develop these pre-writing skills and give children practice in pencil control and fine motor movements before introducing letter formation.

After Book 1b the activities give children the opportunity of looking at and writing words which contain common letter patterns. They teach them to join letters together as early as possible. Lines are not used because they are not necessary for the development of movement and can inhibit the natural flow.

The words used in each book have been selected from the known writing vocabularies of children and are presented in the following age bands:

	Ages	Key Stage	Year Groups
Book 1a, 1b, Phonetic Stage, 2a, 2b	5-7	1	1-2
Books 3a, 3b	7-9	1 & 2	3-4
Books 4a, 4b	9-11	2	5-6

Important Note
With the exception of Book 1a and 1b, which are graded, Books a and b are at the same level. For example, Book 2a begins with one and two-letter patterns, moving through to three and four-letter patterns in Book 2b. Together the two books form a complete resource for Key Stage 1. Books 3a and 3b and 4a and 4b are arranged in the same way.

SELECTING WORKSHEETS

Within each of the books, the worksheets are presented alphabetically, not in order of difficulty. This enables you to select the most appropriate worksheets to meet the needs of the group or individual child. Some worksheets may be needed on more than one occasion.

Some words appear on more than one worksheet. This is either because the letter pattern is repeated across the age ranges with more complex words at a higher level, or because the words contain more than one letter pattern. For example, 'there' appears on the worksheet with 'ere' and the 'the' letter patterns.

The examples below illustrate how worksheets may be selected according to the needs of the group or individual child.

Sam Sed it was his.

This misspelling of 'said' reflects the phonetic stage, that is, there is a match between letter and sound, and 'the alternative is phonetically plausible' (Level Description 2).

The most appropriate approach in this situation is for a child to practise the letter pattern 'sai'. In practising this letter pattern, the movement of the hand through the letters will help the child to 'feel' and then look at other words with a similar structure at the beginning. In this instance, linking 'said' with 'sail' will also help with the visual aspect and discourage reliance on sound.

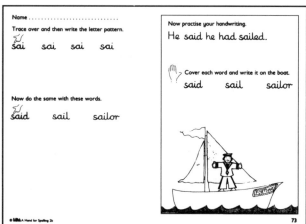

Mum siad it was good.

This misspelling of 'said' reflects the transitional stage, that is, there is evidence of some visual awareness of the letters required for the word 'said'.

The most appropriate approach is to promote the fact that visually 'said' is an 'aid' word. This means relating it to other 'aid' words, for example, 'maid, paid, raid' etc. Although these words also contain the same sound they must be described as 'a-i-d' words. This is a spelling activity, not 'phonetics for reading'. Once again the movement through the word will also help with the visual aspects of the word 'said'.

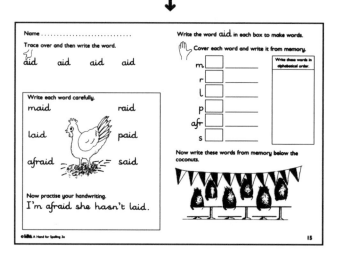

USING THE WORKSHEETS

Each worksheet is designed to give children the opportunity of practising a particular letter pattern in joined writing before moving on to work which focuses on spelling.

On each worksheet there is a mixture of print and joined writing. Instructions, which are for reading, are in print whilst the joined writing, which can also be read, provides the model for handwriting.

Before beginning the worksheet, check the child can read the words. Some children may require help with word recognition and as a result may resort to a phonic approach, that is, decoding. For reading this is perfectly acceptable because 'sounding out' is an important word attack skill. When the child has read (decoded) the word and is asked how to write it the response should be by the names of the letters.

Discuss the formation of the letter pattern. Always use the names of the letters.

This activity helps to cement the letter pattern and the spelling of these words.

Ensure each letter is formed correctly. This may mean continual observation.

Although the sounds are different always describe the pattern as a 'y-o-u' word.

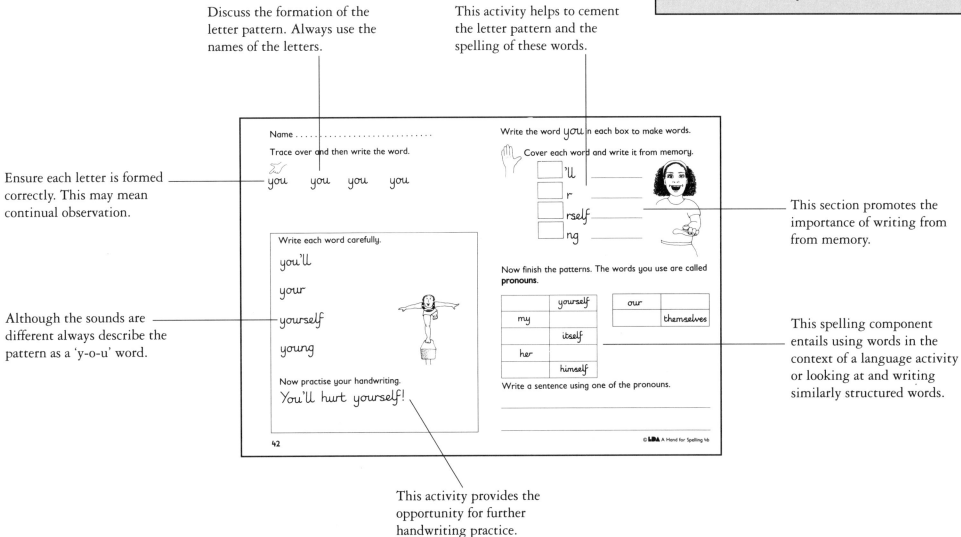

This section promotes the importance of writing from from memory.

This spelling component entails using words in the context of a language activity or looking at and writing similarly structured words.

This activity provides the opportunity for further handwriting practice.

LETTER FORMATION

Some capital letters are used, for example, the personal pronoun 'I' and the letter 'C' as in 'Christmas'. The style recommended for all capital letters is bold print with no join to the lower case letter.

The letters 'g', 'j' and 'y' do not join fully because a fully looped letter can be difficult for young children. This style also encourages the use of some pen lifts how which will be essential for writing with speed later on.

What is important is the movement through the word, so for words containing these letters the procedure is as follows.

▷ If the word begins with a 'g', 'j', or 'y' then it is formed as a single letter, with the following letter beginning from the position it was taught as a single flowing letter.

▷ If the letters 'g', 'j', or 'y' appear within the word then they are joined to the preceding letter in the usual way, but completed as a single letter. The following letter begins from the position it was taught as a single letter.

The apostrophe is used in contractions such as 'didn't' and 'hasn't', hence the reason for its usage will need to be taught.

Check Points

SPELLING

✓ Collect and talk about words containing common letter patterns.

✓ Look for words within words. Visual discrimination of word form is a crucial part of learning how words are structured.

✓ Encourage the 'Look-Cover-Write-Check' routine. Remember that the important aspect of this routine is the writing from memory.

✓ Never ask a child whether a spelling is 'right'. This only promotes the unhelpful notion of 'right and wrong' and is damaging to self image if the word is 'wrong'. Instead, encourage visual inspection of the word by asking, 'Is yours the same as this?' If not, then ask, 'What do you need to do to make it the same?'

✓ Encourage children to verbalise their attempts at difficult words.

✓ Provide opportunities for children to write words in context as well as writing letter patterns.

HANDWRITING

✓ Provide pre-writing activities to promote pencil control.

✓ Teach a pencil grip which is firm but relaxed. The pencil should be held between the thumb and first finger, resting against the middle finger.

✓ Ensure correct posture with children sitting comfortably, with feet flat on the floor and body upright, but tilted slightly forward on a chair suited to the height of the table.

✓ Children should have good light in order to see what they are writing without straining the eye. The writing position should be comfortable and the paper correctly angled to suit either left or right-handers.

✓ Ensure correct letter formation at all times. See pages xiii and xiv for letter formation for both left and right-handed children.

✓ Always encourage movement through the letter pattern or word.

✓ Teach and use letter pattern names and not sounds.

✓ Develop a language of writing which will enable the children to understand and verbalise the physical actions required when writing.

✓ Teach the meanings of words such as: top, bottom, up, down, round, over, back, letter, word, pattern, left, right, join, curved, straight, ascenders, descenders, etc.

✓ Encourage children to discuss the quality of their own handwriting, looking at the letter formation etc.

✓ Encourage children to use different standards of writing for different purposes.

✓ Ensure that children acquire legibility in both print and cursive styles.

✓ Give careful attention to the different needs of left-handed children.

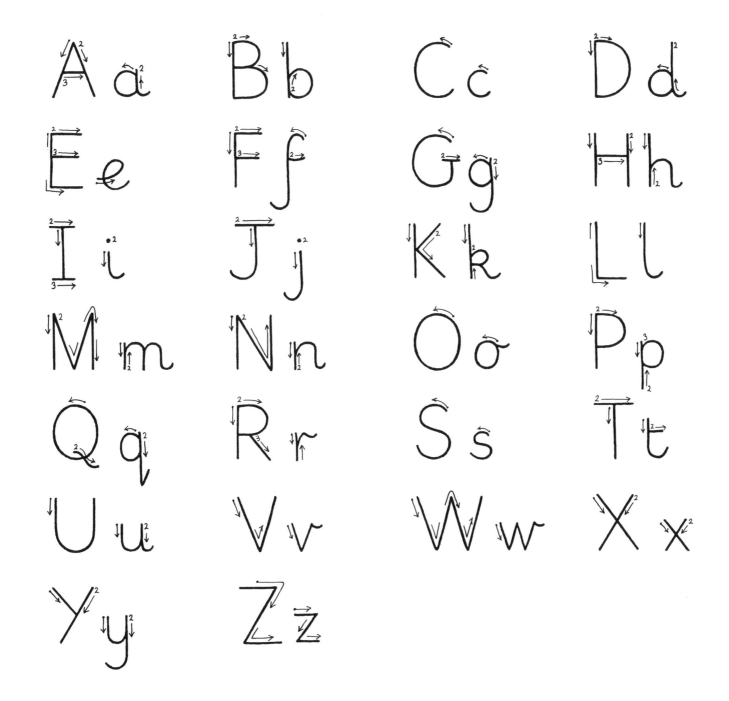

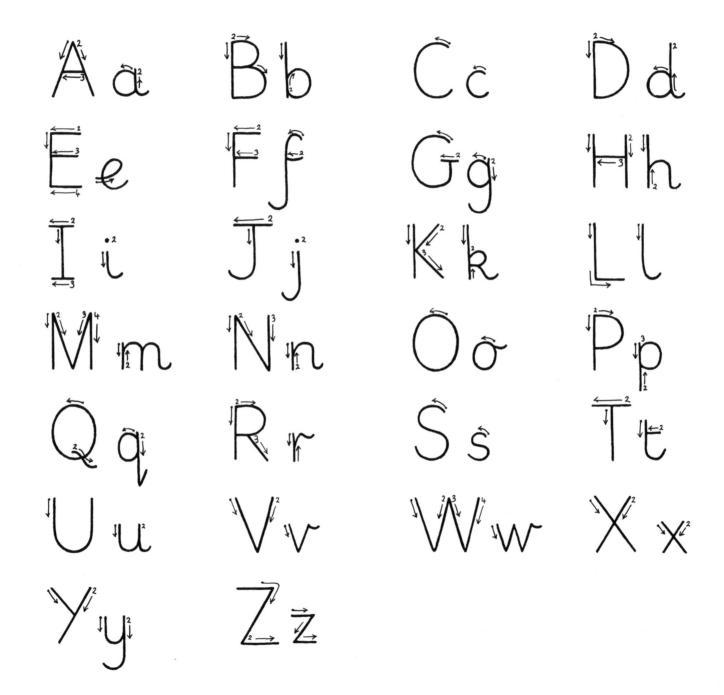

Name . . . .

Trace over and then write the word.

am   am   am   am

Write each word carefully.

damage

exam

gram

tram

diamond

pyjamas

Now practise your handwriting.

pyjamas with diamonds

Write the word am in each box to make words.
Cover each word and write it from memory.

d [ ] age _____

ex [ ] _____

gr [ ] _____

tr [ ] _____

di [ ] ond _____

pyj [ ] as _____

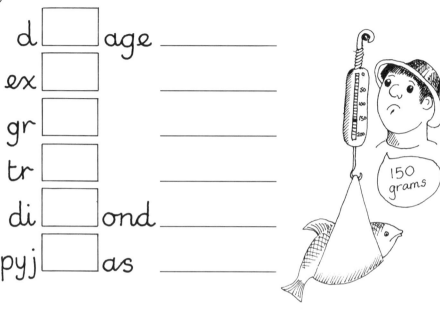

150 grams

Now use these words to finish the dictionary list.

harm or injury   _____

a precious stone   _____

a test   _____

metric unit of   _____
weight

night wear   _____

old fashioned bus   _____

Name . . . .

Trace over and then write the letter pattern.

au   au   au   au

Write each word carefully.

autumn   author   because

sauce   saucer   sausage

Now practise your handwriting.

I like sauce with sausages.

Write the letter pattern au in each box to make words.

Cover each word and write it from memory.

	tumn	_____
	thor	_____
bec	se	_____
s	ce	_____
s	cer	_____
s	sage	_____

Now join up the dots and then answer the questions.

autumn

author

Which word comes first in alphabetical order?

sauce

saucer

sausage

Which word comes last in alphabetical order?

2

Name . . . .

Trace over and then write the letter pattern.

aw   aw   aw   aw

Write each word carefully.

crawl

hawk

lawyer

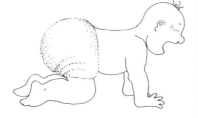

Now practise your handwriting.

The baby crawled and bawled.

Write the letter pattern aw in each box to make words.

 Cover each word and write it from memory.

cr ☐ l _____

h ☐ k _____

l ☐ yer _____

Use aw words to finish the poem.

A creepy _____ caterpillar
_____ along a leaf
A hovering _____ in the sky
_____ him there beneath.
The creepy _____ caterpillar
_____ the _____ and said,
"I'm much too small to make
         a meal,
Keep your _____ away!"

Name . . . .

Trace over and then write the letter pattern.

 ca   ca   ca   ca

Write each word carefully.

cage

cake

came

case

cafe

care

Now practise your handwriting.

We came to have cake at the cafe.

Write the letter pattern ca in each box to make words.

 Cover each word and write it from memory.

	ge	_____
	ke	_____
	me	_____
	se	_____
	fe	_____
	re	_____

Write these words in alphabetical order.

Finish the pattern.

case	
	cakes
cage	
	cafes

Now use came words to finish the sentences.

Smile, please, for the _____ .

He came across the desert on a _____ .

Name . . . .

Trace over and then write the letter pattern.

ea   ea   ea   ea

Write the letter pattern ea in each box to make words.

Cover each word and write it from memory.

	ch	_____
	gle	_____
	sier	_____
	st	_____
	sy	_____
	siest	_____

Write these words in alphabetical order.

Write each word carefully.

each

eagle

easier

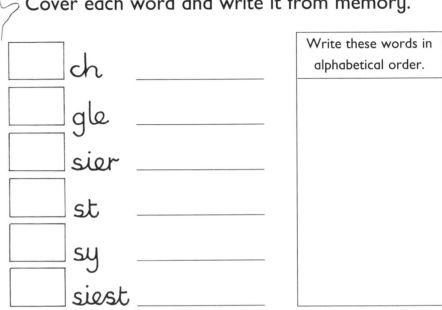

east

easy

easiest

Now practise your handwriting.

The eagle flies east.

Now use some of these words to help you finish the captain's diary.

16 September 1592

Our small ship made an _____ landing on a sandy beach. We carried spades and axes. We turned to the _____ and saw the _____ flying over the mountain. After hacking through the forest we found the going much _____.

Name . . . .

Trace over and then write the letter pattern.

eo　　*eo*　　*eo*　　*eo*

Write the letter pattern *eo* in each box to make words.

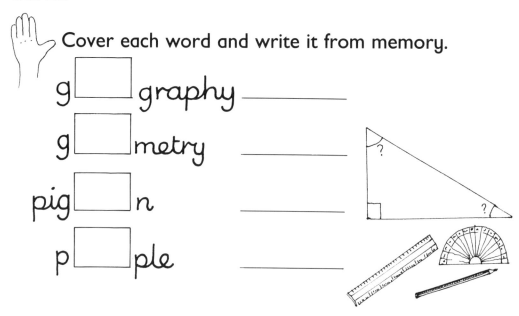

Cover each word and write it from memory.

g [ ] graphy _____

g [ ] metry _____

pig [ ] n _____

p [ ] ple _____

Write each word carefully.

geography　　　　geometry

pigeon　　　　　　people

Now practise your handwriting.

People often feed pigeons.

Now use these words to finish the puzzle.

1. This 'eo' is a study of shapes. [　　]

2. This 'eo' describes more than one person. [　　]

3. This 'eo' is a type of bird. [　　]

4. This 'eo' is a study of places in the world. [　　]

6

Name . . . .

Trace over and then write the letter pattern.

ex   *ex*   *ex*   *ex*

Write each word carefully.

exercise

extra

express

explain

exhibit

index

Now practise your handwriting.

She exhibits her exercises.

Write the letter pattern *ex* in each box to make words.

Cover each word and write it from memory.

[ ] ercise _____

[ ] tra _____

[ ] press _____

[ ] plain _____

[ ] hibit _____

ind [ ] _____

Write these words in alphabetical order.

Find an *ex* word which links with both words in each group.

[   ] bus
             train

[   ] bike
             book

[   ] large
             special

[   ] finger
             number

Name . . . .

Trace over and then write the letter pattern.

kn   kn   kn   kn

Write each word carefully.

knee   knelt   knight

knit   knock   knot

know

Now practise your handwriting.

Knights know how to tie knots.

Write the letter pattern **kn** in each box to make words.

Cover each word and write it from memory.

	ee _____		ock _____
	elt _____		ot _____
	ight _____		ow _____
	it _____		

Finish the pattern.

knit		knitted
	knots	

Use **kn** words to write a sentence about the knight.

_____

_____

© LDA A Hand for Spelling 4a

Name . . . .

Trace over and then write the letter pattern.

oe   oe   oe   oe

Write each word carefully.

hoe

toe

canoe

shoe

poet

poetry

Now practise your handwriting.

The poet wrote a poem.

Write the letter pattern oe in each box to make words.

Cover each word and write it from memory.

h ⬚ _____

t ⬚ _____

can ⬚ _____

sh ⬚ _____

p ⬚ t _____

p ⬚ try _____

This is a picture poem.
Now write your own oe poem and decorate it.

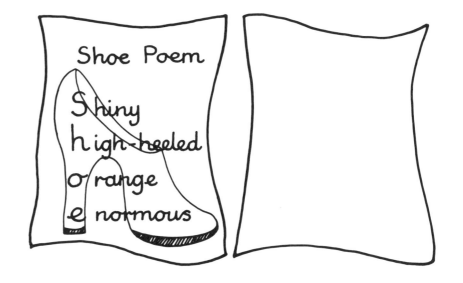

Shoe Poem

Shiny
high-heeled
orange
enormous

Name . . . .

Trace over and then write the letter pattern.

oy   oy   oy   oy

Write each word carefully.

destroy

oysters

toys   boys

Now practise your handwriting.

The boys found an oyster.

Write the letter pattern oy in each box to make words.

Cover each word and write it from memory.

destr ☐ _____

☐ sters _____

t ☐ s _____

b ☐ s _____

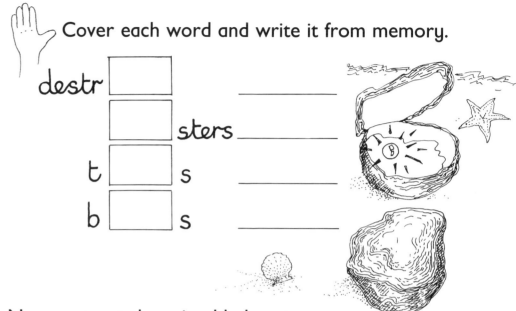

Now sort out these jumbled sentences.

1. boys busy The were their holidays. planning

_____

2. bulldozer destroy the The will building. old

_____

3. oysters The served the first. waiter

_____

4. The were fire. the in toys destroyed

Name . . . .

Trace over and then write the letter pattern.

tw   tw   tw   tw

Write the letter pattern tw in each box to make words.

Cover each word and write it from memory.

be ☐☐ een _____ ☐ elve _____

☐☐ enty _____ ☐ o _____

Now use these tw words to answer the questions.

1. How many 5ps in 10p? ☐

2. How many 5ps in £1? ☐

3. How many in a dozen? ☐

4. Seven comes _____ six and eight. ☐

5. If a ride at the amusement park costs 50p, how many rides can I have for my £1? ☐

Write each word carefully.

between   twelve

twenty   two

1 2 3 4 5 6 7 8 9 10 11 12 13 14 15 16 17 18 19 20

Now practise your handwriting.

Twelve is between two and twenty.

Name . . . .

Trace over and then write the letter pattern.

ue   ue   ue   ue

Write each word carefully.

Tuesday   statue

avenue   value

rescue

Now practise your handwriting.

Coal is a valuable fuel.

Write the letter pattern ue in each box to make words.

Cover each word and write it from memory.

T☐sday _____

aven☐ _____

resc☐ _____

stat☐ _____

val☐ _____

Words that have the same meanings are called **synonyms.** Find ue words that are synonyms to finish the story.

The | monument | | stood in front of the church, at the end of the | road | . When the workmen came to pull it down my friend and I wanted to | save | it.

Trace over and then write the letter pattern.

wr   wr   wr   wr

Write each word carefully.

wrap   wreath   wreck

wrist   write   written

wrong

Ms. S. Wrenshaw,
9, Wretton Street,
Wreham.
RETURN TO SENDER

Now practise your handwriting.

I wrote the wrong address.

Write the letter pattern wr in each box to make words.

Cover each word and write it from memory.

☐ ap _____
☐ eath _____
☐ eck _____
☐ ist _____

☐ ite _____
☐ itten _____
☐ ong _____

Now use some of these words to describe what happened here. Remember to use capital letters and full stops.

_____

_____

_____

_____

Name . . . .

Trace over and then write the letter pattern.

ack   ack   ack   ack

Write each word carefully.

crack

stack

attack

jacket

lack

Now practise your handwriting.

This is the back of a jacket.

Write the letter pattern **ack** in each box to make words.

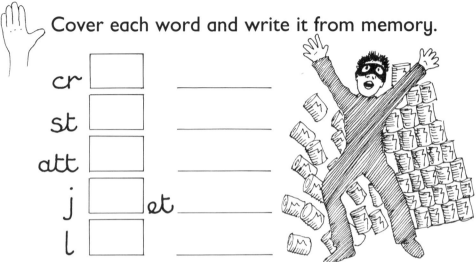

Cover each word and write it from memory.

cr ☐ _____

st ☐ _____

att ☐ _____

j ☐ et _____

l ☐ _____

Now read this story and correct the spelling mistakes.

The robber craked the glass door
and burst into the shop. He backed
into a stack of tins which fell
crashing to the floor. He snached at
the parsels and packages lying about,
but before he could put them into
his bag he was atacked by the
shoppers who caught hold of his
jacket and held him until the
police arrived.

© LDA A Hand for Spelling 4a

Name . . . .

Trace over and then write the word.

 aft   *aft*   *aft*   *aft*

Write each word carefully.

after

afternoon

afterwards

raft

aircraft

Now practise your handwriting.

After lunch he rode on the raft.

Write the word *aft* in each box to make words.

 Cover each word and write it from memory.

☐ er _____

☐ ernoon _____

☐ erwards _____

r ☐ _____

aircr ☐ _____

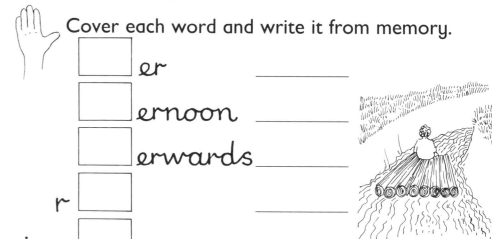

Now use some of these words to finish the crossword.

Across
1. Later than.
4. A word in 'afford'.
5. A hot drink.
6. To see someone.
8. Opposite of high.
9. A plane.
12. A word in 'done'.
13. Exchange something.

Down
1. When something has happened.
2. An enemy.
3. An old fashioned bus.
7. Something special.
8. Someone who tells lies.
10. An animal which gives milk.
11. Mountains in Switzerland.

Name . . . .

Trace over and then write the word.

age   age   age   age

Write each word carefully.

damage

manage

postage

sausage

stage

voyage

Now practise your handwriting.

I can manage another sausage.

Write the word **age** in each box to make words.

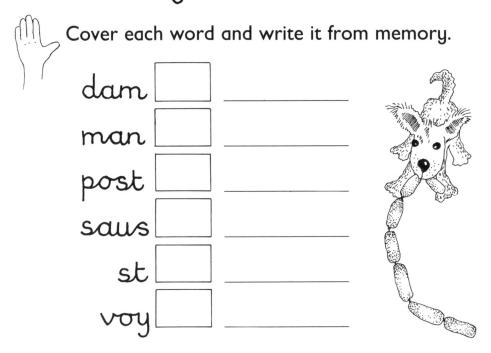

Cover each word and write it from memory.

dam □ _____

man □ _____

post □ _____

saus □ _____

st □ _____

voy □ _____

Now use some of these words and the jigsaw pieces to make pairs of words.

pork   stamp   voyage

sea

postage   stage   sausage   coach

Name . . . .

Trace over and then write the word.

ail   *ail*   *ail*   *ail*

Write each word carefully.

daily   hail

sailor   tailor

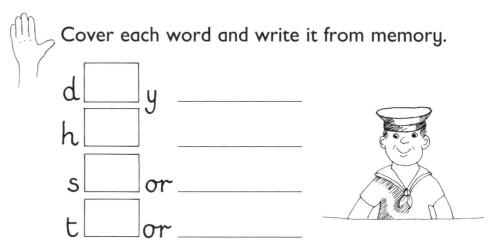

Now practise your handwriting.

tinker, tailor, soldier, sailor

Write the letter pattern *ail* in each box to make words.

Cover each word and write it from memory.

d ☐ y _____

h ☐ _____

s ☐ or _____

t ☐ or _____

Say *tailor*.   Count the number of beats. Tai/lor (2). So tailor has 2 **syllables**. Say and write each *ail* word and count the syllables.

daily ☐ ( )

rail   ☐ ( )

sailor ☐ ( )

tailoring ☐ ( )

trailing ☐ ( )

Name . . . .

Trace over and then write the letter pattern.

ain   ain   ain   ain

Write each word carefully.

against   brain   explain

gain   sprain

plain   rain

Now practise your handwriting.

I explained that I felt faint.

Write the letter pattern **ain** in each box to make words.

Cover each word and write it from memory.

ag[ ]st _____   pl[ ] _____

br[ ] _____   r[ ] _____

expl[ ] _____

g[ ] _____

spr[ ] _____

Say the word <u>explain</u>.
The underlined part is the part you **stress** when you say it. In some dictionaries it is shown by a mark before the stressed part, e.g. ex'plain.
Now write each word and mark the stressed part in the same way.

against [ ]   Britain [ ]

raining [ ]   refrain [ ]

complain [ ]   remain [ ]

Name . . . .

Trace over and then write the letter pattern.

ake   ake   ake   ake

Write each word carefully.

awake

baker

bakery

cake

mistake

Now practise your handwriting.

The baker makes cakes.

Write the letter pattern **ake** in each box to make words.

Cover each word and write it from memory.

aw[ ] _____

b[ ]r _____

b[ ]ry _____

c[ ] _____

mist[ ] _____

Now use some of these words to write a story about a baker who makes a cake which goes wrong. Remember to use capital letters and full stops.

The Surprise Birthday Cake

_____

_____

_____

_____

Name . . . .

Trace over and then write the letter pattern.

ame   ame   ame   ame

Write each word carefully.

name

tame

frame

lame

flame

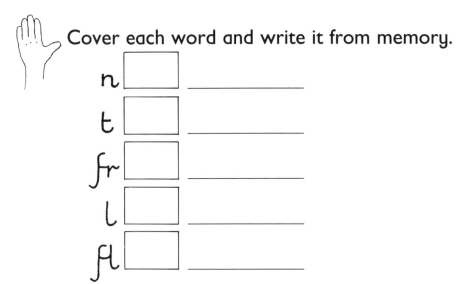

Now practise your handwriting.

They named the tame rabbit.

Write the letter pattern ame in each box to make words.

Cover each word and write it from memory.

n [ ] _____

t [ ] _____

fr [ ] _____

l [ ] _____

fl [ ] _____

Now finish the pattern.

name		
	frames	
		flaming
tame		
	shames	

Now write a sentence using any two of these words.

Name . . . .

Trace over and then write the letter pattern.

ank   ank   ank   ank

Write each word carefully.

ankle

blanket

thanked

Now practise your handwriting.

My ankles stuck out of the blankets.

Write the letter pattern ank in each box to make words.

Cover each word and write it from memory.

☐ le _____

bl ☐ et _____

th ☐ ed _____

Words that have the same meanings are called **synonyms**. Find ank words that are synonyms to finish the sentences.

1. I snuggled under the | cover | |
   hoping the alarm wouldn't ring.
2. They sat on the | slope | | and
   watched the cycle racing in the stadium.
3. There was a wooden | board | |
   leading to the ship.

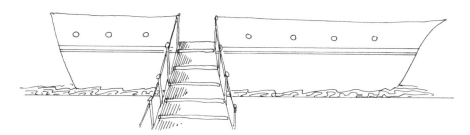

Name . . . .

Trace over and then write the word.

ant   ant   ant   ant

Write each word carefully.

distant   elephant

giant   vacant

Now practise your handwriting.

I want a vacant seat.

Write the word **ant** in each box to make words.

Cover each word and write it from memory.

dist ☐
eleph ☐
gi ☐
vac ☐

Now read through the story and correct the spelling mistakes. Then finish the story.

A Jungle Story

It was a verey strange freindship. The elephent and antelope had lived side by side in the jungle for meny years, but the antelope had stayed distent as he watched the gaint grey creature by the waterhole. Then one day

© LDA A Hand for Spelling 4a

Name . . . .

Trace over and then write the word.

ape   ape   ape   ape

Write each word carefully.

escape

gape

grape

shape

tape

trapeze

Now practise your handwriting.

I made paper shapes.

Write the word **ape** in each box to make words.

Cover each word and write it from memory.

esc ☐ _____

g ☐ _____

gr ☐ _____

sh ☐ _____

t ☐ _____

tr ☐ ze _____

Now use some of these words to finish the poem.

An _____ in a jungle of trees
Used the branches just like a _____.
He esc____d from his foes,
By using his toes.
In a c____ of bright red,
With a cap on his head,
He could have been Batman with ease.

Name . . . .

Trace over and then write the letter pattern.

app   app   app   app

Write the letter pattern **app** in each box to make words.

Cover each word and write it from memory.

☐ ear _____

☐ earance _____

☐ oint _____

☐ reciate _____

dis ☐ ear _____

Now **burst** the words to finish the puzzle.

Write each word carefully.

appear   appearance

appoint   appreciate

disappear

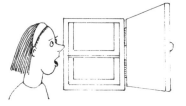

Now practise your handwriting.

It appears to have disappeared.

appointing —— appoint —— appointed

appoints

disappear

appreciate

© LDA A Hand for Spelling 4a

Name . . . .

Trace over and then write the letter pattern.

ara   ara   ara   ara

Write each word carefully.

character

parade

separate

Now practise your handwriting.

The parachutists paraded.

Write the letter pattern **ara** in each box to make words.

Cover each word and write it from memory.

ch [ ] cter _____

p [ ] de _____

sep [ ] te _____

Say parade. Count the number of beats. Pa/rade (2). So parade has two **syllables**. Say and write each ara word and count the syllables.

separate   [   ] ( )

character   [   ] ( )

garage   [   ] ( )

parachute   [   ] ( )

paragraph   [   ] ( )

Name . . . .

Trace over and then write the letter pattern.

ard   ard   ard   ard

Write the letter pattern **ard** in each box to make words.

Cover each word and write it from memory.

c [ ] _____

c [ ] board _____

gu [ ] _____

h [ ] _____

h [ ] ly _____

orch [ ] _____

reg [ ] ed _____

stand [ ] _____

Write each word carefully.

card   cardboard   guard

hard   hardly   orchard

regarded   standard

Now practise your handwriting.

Cards are made from cardboard.

Now print some of these words to fill the boxes.

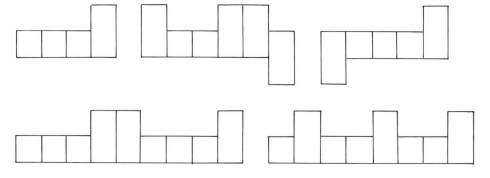

© LDA A Hand for Spelling 4a

Name . . . .

Trace over and then write the word.

are   are   are   are

Write each word carefully.

dare   rare   share

spare   prepare   square

hectare   area

Now practise your handwriting.

A hectare is a square area.

Write the word are in each box to make words.

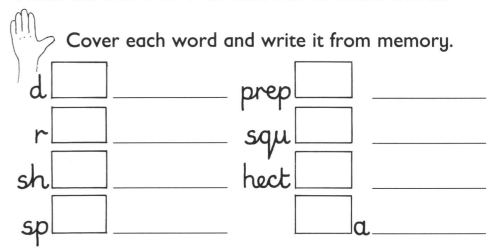

Cover each word and write it from memory.

d ☐ _____   prep ☐ _____

r ☐ _____   squ ☐ _____

sh ☐ _____   hect ☐ _____

sp ☐ _____   ☐ a _____

Now use are words to finish the puzzle.
The letters on the ladder should spell the name of a fruit.

1. Kept in case it is needed.

2. A measure of land.

3. Something unusual.

4. To frighten.

5. Divide into parts.

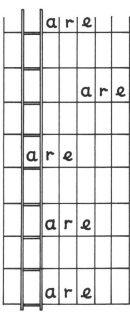

Name . . . .

Trace over and then write the word.

art   art   art   art

Write each word carefully.

article

artist

chart

quarter

Now practise your handwriting.

The artist paints a chart.

Write the word art in each box to make words.

Cover each word and write it from memory.

□ icle _____

□ ist _____

ch □ _____

qu □ er _____

Now use art words to fill the boxes.

one of four equal parts

someone who draws or paints

belonging to something bigger

a particular thing

dressed well, or stinging pain

a map or paper with information on

Name . . . .

Trace over and then write the letter pattern.

ary   ary   ary   ary

Write each word carefully.

canary

library

dictionary

secretary

necessary

stationary

Now practise your handwriting.

A dictionary may be necessary.

Write the letter pattern ary in each box to make words.

Cover each word and write it from memory.

can ☐ _____   secret ☐ _____

libr ☐ _____   necess ☐ _____

diction ☐ _____   station ☐ _____

Now finish the pattern.

canary	
	secretaries
library	
	dictionaries

Use ary words to finish the poem.

Sometimes I get stuck

On a word like '_____',

Then I find it _____

To find it in a _____.

Name . . . .

Trace over and then write the letter pattern.

ase   *ase*   *ase*   *ase*

Write each word carefully.

base   case

chase   phrase

vase

Now practise your handwriting.

The base of the vase was cracked.

Write the letter pattern *ase* in each box to make words.

 Cover each word and write it from memory.

b [ ] _____

c [ ] _____

ch [ ] _____

phr [ ] _____

v [ ] _____

Now use these words to make other *ase* words.

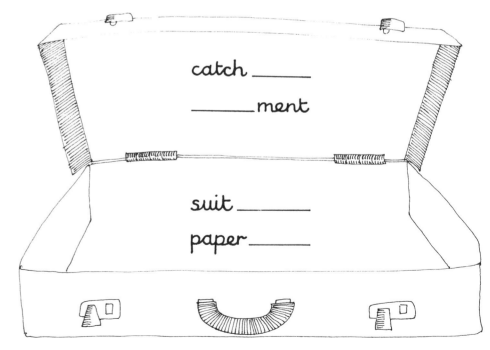

catch_____

_____ment

suit_____

paper_____

© LDA A Hand for Spelling 4a

Name . . . .

Trace over and then write the word.

ash   ash   ash   ash

Write each word carefully.

ashore

ashamed

ashes

lash

flash

splash

Now practise your handwriting.

In a flash she splashed ashore.

Write the word ash in each box to make words.

Cover each word and write it from memory.

☐ ore _____

☐ amed _____

☐ es _____

l ☐ _____

fl ☐ _____

spl ☐ _____

Write these words in alphabetical order.

Now use ash words to finish the story.

Grace Darling watched the storm from the cottage window. Lightning _____ across the darkness and cold rain needled the windows. Wind _____ the waves to a white fury. Beyond the cliffs the passenger boat she had seen earlier in the day struggled against the storm. Would its passengers ever come _____?

Name . . . .

Trace over and then write the word.

ass   *ass*   *ass*   *ass*

Write the word *ass* in each box to make words.

Cover each word and write it from memory.

br [ ] _____

gl [ ] es _____

gr [ ] _____

p [ ] _____

[ ] embly _____

p [ ] enger _____

Write each word carefully.

brass

glasses

grass

pass

assembly

passenger

Now practise your handwriting.

He passed me a glass.

Now finish the pattern.

brass		
	grassy	
		passes
glass		
lass		

Name . . . .

Trace over and then write the letter pattern.

ato   *ato*   *ato*   *ato*

Write each word carefully.

tomato

potato

atom

Now practise your handwriting.

I like tomatoes and potatoes.

Write the letter pattern **ato** in each box to make words.

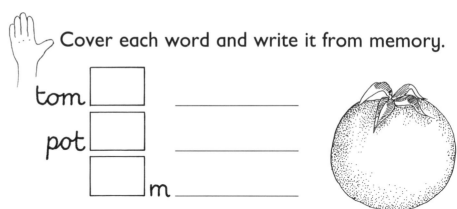 Cover each word and write it from memory.

tom ☐ _____

pot ☐ _____

☐ m _____

Find an **ato** word which links with the word before and the word after it.

baked _____ crisps

tinned _____ sauce

Now finish the pattern.

tomato	
	potatoes

Name . . . .

Trace over and then write the letter pattern.

ave   ave   ave   ave

Write each word carefully.

behave

grave

gravel

haven't

traveller

loaves

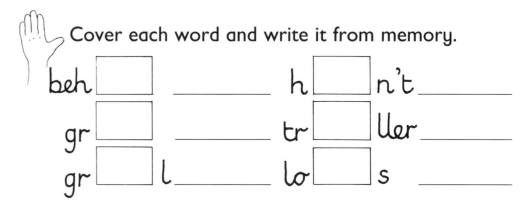

Now practise your handwriting.

The traveller was brave.

Write the letter pattern ave in each box to make words.

✋ Cover each word and write it from memory.

beh☐ _____   h☐n't _____

gr☐ _____   tr☐ller _____

gr☐l _____   lo☐s _____

Words that have the same meanings are called **synonyms**. Now use ave words that are synonyms to finish the story. Give your answer to the question at the end.

The ☐explorer☐ faced many dangers. At night he heard and felt the animals close by him in the jungle. He tried always to ☐act☐ in a ☐courageous☐ way. He battled on, always thinking about the animal he had come to ☐rescue☐. What do you think it was?

© LDA A Hand for Spelling 4a

Name . . . .

Trace over and then write the word.

bar   bar   bar   bar

Write each word carefully.

barley

barred

barrel

bare

Now practise your handwriting.

The barley is in the barn.

Write the word **bar** in each box to make words.

Cover each word and write it from memory.

☐ ley _____

☐ red _____

☐ rel _____

☐ e _____

Now use these words to finish the puzzles.

1. A crop grown by farmers.

2. Without clothes or covering.

3. A round wooden container or part of a gun.

4. Prevented.

Name . . . .

Trace over and then write the letter pattern.

ber   ber   ber   ber

Write each word carefully.

September   October

November   December

iceberg

Now practise your handwriting.

Remember the months of the year.

Write the letter pattern *ber* in each box to make words.

Cover each word and write it from memory.

Septem ☐ _____

Octo ☐ _____

Novem ☐ _____

Decem ☐ _____

ice ☐ g _____

Now use some of these words to complete the calendar pages.

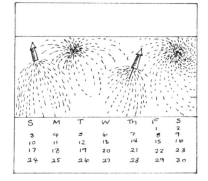
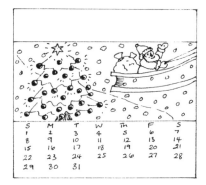

Name . . . .

Trace over and then write the letter pattern.

bur   bur   bur   bur

Write each word carefully.

burn   burst

bury   buried

Now practise your handwriting.

The burglar buried his loot.

Write the letter pattern bur in each box to make words.

Cover each word and write it from memory.

☐ n _____

☐ st _____

☐ y _____

☐ ied _____

Write these words in alphabetical order.

Now sort out these jumbled sentences.

1. tyre loud The car with bang. a burst

_____

2. king buried The the in was cathedral.

_____

3. to the David burn rubbish. began

_____

4. said bury treasure in the would
Susan she garden. the

_____

_____

Name . . . .

Trace over and then write the word.

car   car   car   car

Write each word carefully.

cart

carpenter

caravan

caring

scar

scared

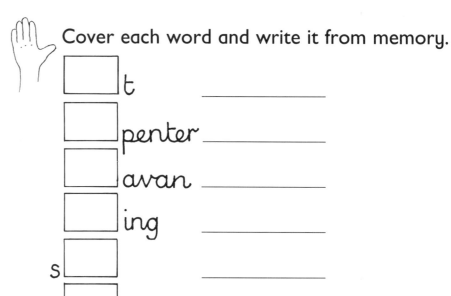

Now practise your handwriting.

The car tows the caravan.

Write the word car in each box to make words.

Cover each word and write it from memory.

☐ t   _____

☐ penter   _____

☐ avan   _____

☐ ing   _____

s ☐   _____

s ☐ ed   _____

Now finish the story using car words instead of pictures.

On our journey, we saw some things being towed. First we passed a tractor pulling a farm  , then a pulling a  . The  was wobbling about and I was . But we managed to overtake.

Name . . . .

Trace over and then write the letter pattern.

cei   *cei*   *cei*   *cei*

Write each word carefully.

receive

receipt

ceiling

Now practise your handwriting.

He's coming through the ceiling.

Write the letter pattern *cei* in each box to make words.

 Cover each word and write it from memory.

re ⬜ ve _____

re ⬜ pt _____

⬜ ling _____

How many *cei* words can you circle in the word search?

r	h	i	o	s	p	t	a	l	m
e	i	g	h	t	k	s	b	c	l
e	a	c	r	e	c	e	i	p	t
c	e	l	i	n	g	e	c	t	s
e	s	r	e	c	e	i	v	e	g
r	e	c	i	v	e	n	t	u	r
c	e	l	c	e	i	l	i	n	g
e	n	d	e	i	l	i	g	e	s

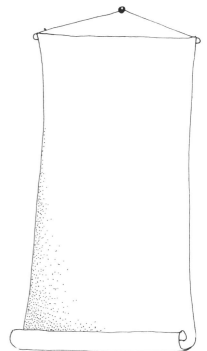

Name . . . .

Trace over and then write the letter pattern.

cho   cho   cho   cho

Write each word carefully.

chose

choose

chocolate

choir

chorus

Now practise your handwriting.

The choir sang a chorus.

Write the letter pattern cho in each box to make words.

Cover each word and write it from memory.

[ ] se _____

[ ] ose _____

[ ] colate _____

[ ] ir _____

[ ] rus _____

Write these words in alphabetical order.

Finish the sentence using cho words.

Would you _____ toffee or _____?

Choose a name for the chocolate bar and design a wrapper.

Name . . . .

Trace over and then write the letter pattern.

coa   coa   coa   coa

Write each word carefully.

coach   coast

coat   cocoa

Now practise your handwriting.

We drank cocoa on the coach.

Write the letter pattern coa in each box to make words.

Cover each word and write it from memory.

☐ ch _____

☐ st _____

☐ t _____

co ☐ _____

Write a coa word to rhyme with each of these.

toast _____

poach _____

boat _____

Now find the coa word that links with the word before and the word after it.

rain ☐ hanger
sea ☐ guard
football ☐ trip
hot ☐ beans

Name . . . .

Trace over and then write the letter pattern.

con   con   con   con

Write each word carefully.

concert

concrete

condition

consider

contain

continent

continue

Now practise your handwriting.

Concrete contains sand and cement.

Write the letter pattern con in each box to make words.

Cover each word and write it from memory.

	cert	_____
	crete	_____
	dition	_____
	sider	_____
	tain	_____
	tinent	_____
	tinue	_____

Say concrete . Count the number of beats.
Con/crete (2). So concrete has two **syllables**.
Say and write each word and count the syllables

concert		( )
condition		( )
consider		( )
continent		( )

Name . . . .

Trace over and then write the letter pattern.

cou   cou   cou   cou

Write each word carefully.

council

count

could

cough

cousin

course

Now practise your handwriting.

My cousin had a cough.

Write the letter pattern **cou** in each box to make words.

Cover each word and write it from memory.

☐ ncil _____

☐ nt _____

☐ ld _____

☐ gh _____

☐ sin _____

☐ rse _____

Write these words in alphabetical order.

Now finish the sentence with a **cou** word.
Some words may need a plural 's' or an 'ed' ending.

1. My _____ and my aunt came to visit.
2. Most of my class were ill with _____ and colds.
3. Our dustbins were emptied by the _____ lorry.
4. When I _____,there were a hundred.

Name . . . .

Trace over and then write the letter pattern.

dge   dge   dge   dge

Write each word carefully.

badge

edge

judge

ledge

ridge

knowledge

Now practise your handwriting.

He was on the edge of the ledge.

Write the letter pattern dge in each box to make words.

Cover each word and write it from memory.

ba ☐ _____

e ☐ _____

ju ☐ _____

le ☐ _____

ri ☐ _____

knowle ☐ _____

Find an dge word that links with each group.

high ⎫
narrow ⎬ _____
shelf ⎭

name ⎫
pinned ⎬ _____
label ⎭

facts ⎫
information ⎬ _____
remember ⎭

courtroom ⎫
wig ⎬ _____
trial ⎭

Trace over and then write the letter pattern.

dom   *dom*   *dom*   *dom*

Write each word carefully.

freedom

kingdom

seldom

wisdom

Now practise your handwriting.

He ruled his kingdom with wisdom.

Write the letter pattern **dom** in each box to make words.

Cover each word and write it from memory.

free ☐ _____

king ☐ _____

sel ☐ _____

wis ☐ _____

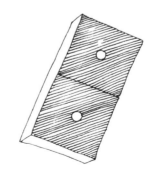

Now crack the code and write the words.

a	b	c	d	e	f	g	h	i	j	k	l	m	n	o	p	q	r	s	t	u	v	w	x	y	z
z	y	x	w	v	u	t	s	r	q	p	o	n	m	l	k	j	i	h	g	f	e	d	c	b	a

d r h w l n ☐

h v o w l n ☐

w l n v ☐

w l n r m l ☐

u i v w l n ☐

Name . . . .

Trace over and then write the letter pattern.

ead   *ead*   *ead*   *ead*

Write each word carefully.

bread   dread

instead   steady

leader

Now practise your handwriting.

He held the bread steady.

Write the letter pattern *ead* in each box to make words.

Cover each word and write it from memory.

br ☐ _____

dr ☐ _____

inst ☐ _____

st ☐ y _____

l ☐ er _____

Now use some of these *ead* words and the jigsaw pieces to make new words.

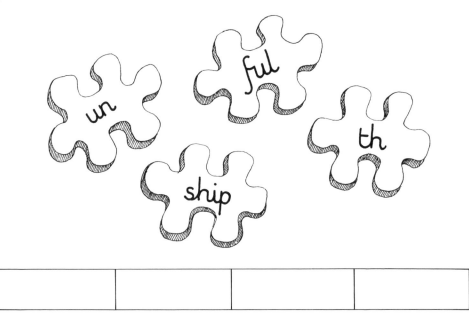

Name . . . .

Trace over and then write the letter pattern.

 *eal* *eal* *eal* *eal*

Write each word carefully.

meal

real

steal

healthy

jealous

wealth

Now practise your handwriting.

I had a really good meal.

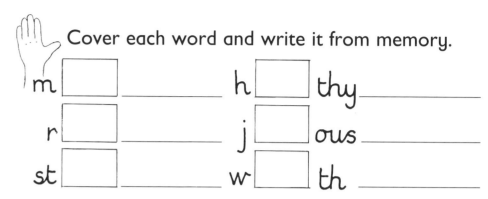

Write the letter pattern *eal* in each box to make words.

Cover each word and write it from memory.

m ☐ _____   h ☐ thy _____

r ☐ _____   j ☐ ous _____

st ☐ _____   w ☐ th _____

This is an **acrostic** poem. The first letters of each line spell another word which is also linked to the poem. Now write your own **acrostic** poem.

M enu

e ating

a pples

l emonade

H
e
a
l
t
h
y

Name . . . .

Trace over and then write the letter pattern.

ean   *ean*   *ean*   *ean*

Write each word carefully.

bean   mean

meanwhile   meant

Now practise your handwriting.
I meant to have beans.

Write the letter pattern *ean* in each box to make words.

Cover each word and write it from memory.

b ☐ _____

m ☐ _____

m ☐ while _____

m ☐ t _____

Now find all the *ean* words.

koceanqumeantwebeanormeaningnmeanteameanwhile

Now write a sentence using any two of these words.

_____

_____

Name . . . .

Trace over and then write the word.

ear   *ear*   *ear*   *ear*

Write each word carefully.

appear

fear

nearly

early

learned

search

LOST
wearing
a blue collar

REWARD
OFFERED

Now practise your handwriting.

I fear he's disappeared.

Write the word *ear* in each box to make words.

Cover each word and write it from memory.

app ☐ _____

f ☐ _____

n ☐ ly _____

☐ ly _____

l ☐ ned _____

s ☐ ch _____

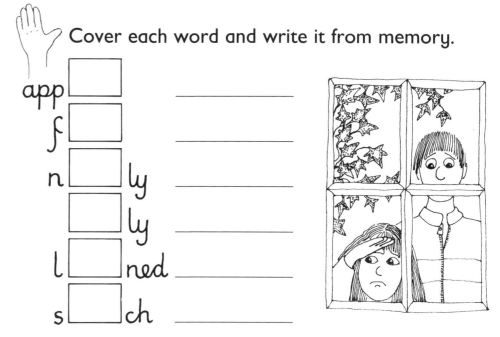

Now read this story and correct the spelling mistakes.

When we got back from Londin, Tim had
dissappeared. We serched in the shed where he
usualy goes but he wasn't there. After two days
we feered he'd been run over, but early one day he
scratcht at the door. He was dirty and thin.
After a tin of sardines he was nearly his old self.
Tim is our _____ of course.

Name . . . .

Trace over and then write the letter pattern.

eas   *eas*   *eas*   *eas*

Write the letter pattern *eas* in each box to make words.

Cover each word and write it from memory.

	y	_____
m	les	_____
s	on	_____
t	poon	_____
m	ure	_____
pl	ure	_____

Write these words in alphabetical order.

Write each word carefully.

easy   *measles*   *season*

teaspoon   *measure*   *pleasure*

Now practise your handwriting.

Measure with a teaspoon.

Say each of the words below. Find *eas* words that sound the same.

treasure

reason

weasels

Name . . . .

Trace over and then write the word.

eat   eat   eat   eat

Write each word carefully.

heat

wheat

breath

leather

weather

theatre

Now practise your handwriting.

I can't breathe in this heat.

Write the word *eat* in each box to make words.

Cover each word and write it from memory.

h ☐ _____

wh ☐ _____

br ☐ h _____

l ☐ her _____

w ☐ her _____

th ☐ re _____

Now find the small words in the following words.

weather	theatre

theatre – at = _____

Name . . . .

Trace over and then write the letter pattern.

eck   *eck*   *eck*   *eck*

Write each word carefully.

deck   neck

speck   wreck

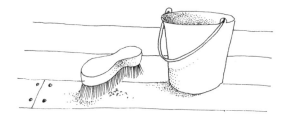

Now practise your handwriting.

no speck on the deck

Write the letter pattern *eck* in each box to make words.

 Cover each word and write it from memory.

d [ ] _____   n [ ] _____

sp [ ] _____   wr [ ] _____

Now rewrite the sentences using *eck* words with an apostrophe and an 's'.

1. The ship's _____ was scrubbed every day. _____

_____

2. The footballer's _____ was very stiff. _____

_____

3. The driver's _____ car was towed away. _____

_____

© LDA A Hand for Spelling 4a

Trace over and then write the letter pattern.

ect   ect   ect   ect

Write each word carefully.

collect   object

perfect   project

respect   electricity

Now practise your handwriting.

He collected the projector.

Write the letter pattern *ect* in each box to make words.

Cover each word and write it from memory.

coll ☐ _____

obj ☐ _____

perf ☐ _____

proj ☐ _____

resp ☐ _____

el ☐ ricity _____

Now add *or* to make new words.

project ☐

object ☐

collect ☐

visit ☐

elect ☐

Name . . . .

Trace over and then write the letter pattern.

eer   *eer*   *eer*   *eer*

Write each word carefully.

steer   cheerful

engineer   pioneer

Now practise your handwriting.

The cheerful pioneer steered.

Write the letter pattern *eer* in each box to make words.

Cover each word and write it from memory.

st ☐ _____

ch ☐ ful _____

engin ☐ _____

pion ☐ _____

Now read the story and correct the spelling mistakes.

On the school trip to France we were taken on a tour of the ferry by the captian. In the depths of the ship we met a cheerfull enginear who showed us the shining new diesel engines. Later our techer was given a chance to steer the boat.

Name . . . .

Trace over and then write the word.

end　　*end*　　*end*　　*end*

Write each word carefully.

attend

friend

spending

splendid

calendar

independent

December

S	M	T	W	Th	F	S
					1	2	3
4	5	6	7	8	9	10
11	12	13	14	15	16	17
18	19	20	21	22	23	24
25	26	27	28	29	30	31

Now practise your handwriting.

The calendar has ended.

Write the word *end* in each box to make words.

Cover each word and write it from memory.

att⬜ _____

fri⬜ _____

sp⬜ing _____

spl⬜id _____

cal⬜ar _____

indep⬜ent _____

Now find the small words in the following words.

spending	independent	calendar

Name . . . .

Trace over and then write the letter pattern.

ent   ent   ent   ent

Write each word carefully.

current

gentle

prevent

silent

entertain

excellent

Now practise your handwriting.

The entertainment was excellent.

Write the letter pattern *ent* in each box to make words.

Cover each word and write it from memory.

curr [ ]   _____

g [ ] le   _____

prev [ ]   _____

sil [ ]   _____

[ ] ertain   _____

excell [ ]   _____

Now use some of these words to finish the story. Then underline any new *ent* words you can find.

Plenty of people came. There were mums, dads, brothers and sisters. We were all _____ when the choir sang the opening song but we clapped and cheered later. The _____ment was very enjoyable and we all agreed it had been an _____ event.

Trace over and then write the letter pattern.

ept   *ept*   *ept*   *ept*

Write each word carefully.

crept

kept

swept

Now practise your handwriting.

She crept in and kept the cheese.

Write the letter pattern *ept* in each box to make words.

 Cover each word and write it from memory.

cr ☐ _____

k ☐ _____

sw ☐ _____

Now finish the pattern.

keep	
	crept
sweep	
	slept

Now fill in the missing words.

1. The opposite of gave is _____.

2. The opposite of woke is _____.

Name . . . .

Trace over and then write the letter pattern.

ery   *ery*   *ery*   *ery*

Write each word carefully.

celery

embroidery

machinery

mystery

slippery

stationery

Now practise your handwriting.

I'm very fond of celery.

Write the letter pattern *ery* in each box to make words.

Cover each word and write it from memory.

cel ☐ _____

embroid ☐ _____

machin ☐ _____

myst ☐ _____

slipp ☐ _____

station ☐ _____

Now use some of these words to finish the dictionary list. Add meanings if they are missing.

e _____	_____
_____	engines
m _____	_____
_____	shiny and smooth
_____	writing paper

Name . . . .

Trace over and then write the word.

eve   eve   eve   eve

Write each word carefully.

develop

ever

level

never

evening

fever

Now practise your handwriting.

The fever developed that evening.

Write the word eve in each box to make words.

Cover each word and write it from memory.

d [ ] lop _____   n [ ] r _____

[ ] r _____   [ ] ning _____

l [ ] l _____   f [ ] r _____

Now find a word which means the same as the phrase.

1. Not ever. [ ]

2. The end of the day. [ ]

3. Flat and smooth. [ ]

4. At any time. [ ]

5. Illness and high temperature. [ ]

6. Grow or change. [ ]

Name . . . .

Trace over and then write the letter pattern.

fif   fif   fif   fif

Write each word carefully.

fifteen

fifth

fifty

Now practise your handwriting.

She'll be fifteen on the fifth.

Write the letter pattern fif in each box to make words.

Cover each word and write it from memory.

☐ teen   _____

☐ th   _____

☐ ty   _____

Now burst the words to finish the puzzle.

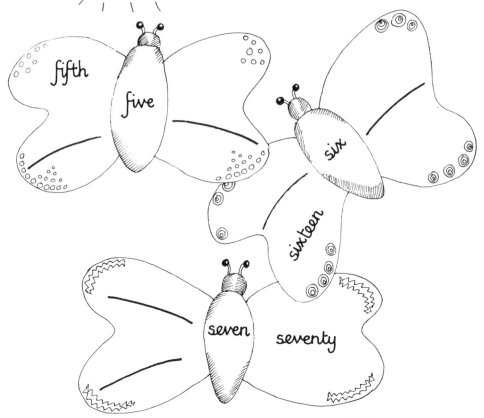

fifth   five   six   sixteen   seven   seventy

Name . . . .

Trace over and then write the word.

for   for   for   for

Write each word carefully.

force   ford   forgive

forgotten   fort   forwards

foreign   forest

Now practise your handwriting.

We forgot our way in the forest.

Write the word for in each box to make words.

Cover each word and write it from memory.

☐ ce	_____
☐ d	_____
☐ give	_____
☐ gotten	_____
☐ t	_____
☐ wards	_____
☐ eign	_____
☐ est	_____

Write three sentences about a computer game using for words.

1. _____

2. _____

3. _____

Name . . . .

Trace over and then write the letter pattern.

fri   *fri*   *fri*   *fri*

Write each word carefully.

friend

fright

fringe

Now practise your handwriting.

My friend's fringe is too long.

Write the letter pattern *fri* in each box to make words.

Cover each word and write it from memory.

☐ end _____

☐ ght _____

☐ nge _____

Now underline the *fri* and *end* patterns in the sentence below.

I'll see my friend on Friday,
just before the weekend.

Now write some funny sayings to help you remember fright and friend.

_____

_____

_____

Name . . . .

Trace over and then write the letter pattern.

ful   ful   ful   ful

Write each word carefully.

beautiful
careful
graceful
handful
playful
thoughtful

Now practise your handwriting.

a beautiful, graceful dancer

Write the letter pattern ful in each box to make words.

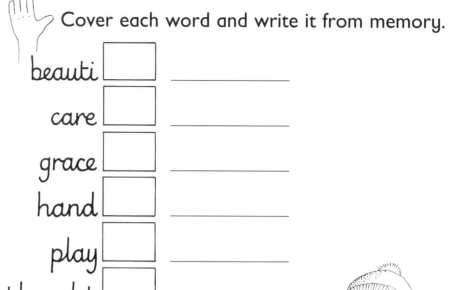

Cover each word and write it from memory.

beauti ☐ _____

care ☐ _____

grace ☐ _____

hand ☐ _____

play ☐ _____

thought ☐ _____

Now finish the pattern.

	handful
care	
	thoughtful
teaspoon	
	pocketful

Name . . . .

Trace over and then write the word.

fur   *fur*   *fur*   *fur*

Write the word *fur* in each box to make words.

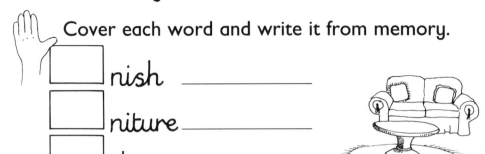

Cover each word and write it from memory.

[ ] nish _____

[ ] niture _____

[ ] ther _____

Write each word carefully.

furnish

furniture

further

FURRY'S REMOVALS

Now practise your handwriting.

They're moving *further* away.

Now print these words to fill the boxes.

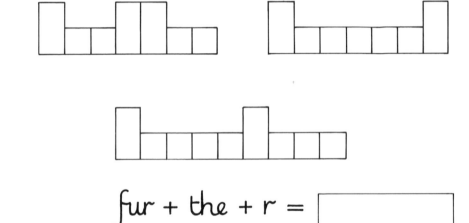

fur + *the* + *r* = [   ]

Now write a sentence using any two of these words.

_____

_____

Name . . . .

Trace over and then write the letter pattern.

gen   gen   gen   gen

Write each word carefully.

general

generation

gentle

intelligent

oxygen

Now practise your handwriting.

The general is intelligent.

Write the letter pattern gen in each box to make words.

Cover each word and write it from memory.

☐ eral _____

☐ eration _____

☐ tle _____

intelli ☐ t _____

oxy ☐ _____

Now use gen words to finish the puzzles.

1. I'm a gas we need to stay alive.

2. I'm kind and calm.

3. I'm an important officer in the army.

4. I'm very clever.

5. I'm a group of people born at the same time.

6. I'm Aladdin's friend from the lamp.

Name . . . .

Trace over and then write the letter pattern.

geo   geo   geo   geo

Write each word carefully.

geography

geometry

pigeon

Now practise your handwriting.

Georgina likes geography.

Write the letter pattern geo in each box to make words.

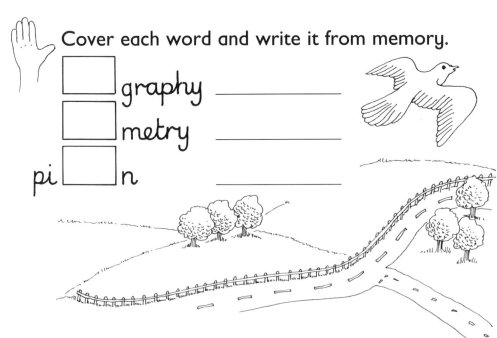

Cover each word and write it from memory.

☐ graphy _____

☐ metry _____

pi ☐ n _____

Now underline all the geo words in this poem.

How does a pigeon fly
When he leaves his garden shed?
Does he understand geography
Somewhere inside his head?
Or does he use geometry
As he soars across the sky,
In a maze of lines and angles
That he sees with his keen eye?

Name . . . .

Trace over and then write the word.

get   *get*   *get*   *get*

Write each word carefully.

target

together

altogether

Now practise your handwriting.

We'll get together tomorrow.

Write the word **get** in each box to make words.

 Cover each word and write it from memory.

tar [ ] _____

to [ ] her _____

alto [ ] her _____

The black letters are called **vowels**.
The others are called consonants.

a b c d **e** f g h **i** j k l m n **o** p q r s t **u** v w x y z

Now find the vowels to finish the words.

_lt_g_th_r   [ ]

f_rg_t   [ ]

t_rg_t   [ ]

t_g_th_r   [ ]

Name . . . .

Trace over and then write the letter pattern.

gue   gue   gue   gue

Write each word carefully.

guess

guessed

guest

league

tongue

Now practise your handwriting.

She put her tongue out.

Write the letter pattern gue in each box to make words.

Cover each word and write it from memory.

☐ ss _____   lea ☐ _____

☐ ssed _____   ton ☐ _____

☐ st _____

Now sort out these jumbled sentences.

1. guess names He the of the tried guests. to

_____

2. burnt the tongue. girl's soup The hot

_____

3. the team of league. top The was school

_____

Name . . . .

Trace over and then write the word.

ice   ice   ice   ice

Write each word carefully.

advice   price   spice

justice   notice   practice

service   police

Now practise your handwriting.

Sugar and spice are very nice.

Write the word *ice* in each box to make words.

Cover each word and write it from memory.

adv ☐ _____

pr ☐ _____

sp ☐ _____

just ☐ _____

not ☐ _____

pract ☐ _____

serv ☐ _____

pol ☐ _____

netball

board

tag

station

free

Now use some of these words and the jigsaw pieces to make pairs of words.

Name . . . .

Trace over and then write the letter pattern.

ide   *ide*   *ide*   *ide*

Write each word carefully.

aside

decide

hide

provide

tide

consider

Now practise your handwriting.

Bride and groom stride away.

Write the letter pattern **ide** in each box to make words.

Cover each word and write it from memory.

as ☐ _____

dec ☐ _____

h ☐ _____

prov ☐ _____

t ☐ _____

cons ☐ r _____

Now finish the pattern.

provide			providing
	decides		
		divided	

Now write a sentence using any two of these words.

Name . . . .

Trace over and then write the letter pattern.

ied   *ied*   *ied*   *ied*

Write each word carefully.

cried   fried

satisfied   tried

Now practise your handwriting.

A fried breakfast satisfied him.

Write the letter pattern *ied* in each box to make words.

Cover each word and write it from memory.

cr ☐ _____

fr ☐ _____

satisf ☐ _____

tr ☐ _____

Now finish the pattern.

spy			
	cries		
		tried	
			frying
satisfy			

Now use some of these words to finish the sentences.

1. Would you like _____ or boiled eggs?
2. I _____ when I broke my arm.

Name . . . .

Trace over and then write the letter pattern.

iff   *iff*   *iff*   *iff*

Write each word carefully.

cliff   *stiff*   *difficult*

Now practise your handwriting.

The cliff was difficult to climb.

Write the letter pattern *iff* in each box to make words.

Cover each word and write it from memory.

cl [ ] _____

st [ ] _____

d [ ] icult _____

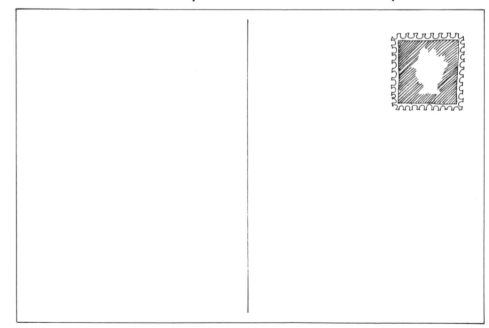

Now send a postcard to a friend describing the climbers you saw on the cliff.
Use some of the *iff* words.

Remember to use capital letters and full stops.

Name . . . .

Trace over and then write the letter pattern.

ift   ift   ift   ift

Write each word carefully.

drift   rift

swift   thrifty

Now practise your handwriting.

The swift drifts on the breeze.

Write the letter pattern *ift* in each box to make words.

Cover each word and write it from memory.

dr [ ] _____

r [ ] _____

sw [ ] _____

thr [ ] y _____

Find the *ift* word that links with each phrase.

1. careful with money   [   ]

2. quick, or a bird   [   ]

3. a crack in the earth   [   ]

4. wander along   [   ]

Name . . . .

Trace over and then write the letter pattern.

imb   imb   imb   imb

Write each word carefully.

limb   timber

climb   climber

Now practise your handwriting.

The climber risked life and limb.

Write the letter pattern imb in each box to make words.

Cover each word and write it from memory.

l ☐ _____

t ☐ er _____

c ☐ _____

c ☐ er _____

Now find a word which means the same as the phrase.

1. wood or trees   ☐

2. arm or leg   ☐

3. to move upwards   ☐

4. person who goes upwards ☐

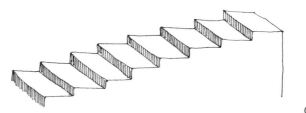

Name . . . .

Trace over and then write the letter pattern.

ind   ind   ind   ind

Write each word carefully.

blind

remind

indeed

index

window

Now practise your handwriting.

The window has a blind.

Write the letter pattern **ind** in each box to make words.

Cover each word and write it from memory.

bl[ ] _____

rem[ ] _____

[ ]eed _____

[ ]ex _____

w[ ]ow _____

Write these words in alphabetical order.

Now find the small words in the following words.

reminder	window	indicator

Find the **ind** words to go with each word.

_____ fold   _____ card

_____ frame

Name . . . .

Trace over and then write the letter pattern.

ine   *ine*   *ine*   *ine*

Write the letter pattern **ine** in each box to make words.

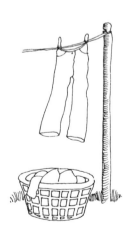

Cover each word and write it from memory.

m ☐ r _____

eng ☐ _____

v ☐ gar _____

cab ☐ t _____

mach ☐ _____

magaz ☐ _____

Now add **s** to the words to make plurals.

miner	miners
engine	
cabinet	
magazine	
machine	
line	

Write each word carefully.

miner   engine

vinegar   cabinet

machine   magazine

Now practise your handwriting.

The engineer fixed the machine.

Name . . . .

Trace over and then write the word.

ink   *ink*   *ink*   *ink*

Write the word *ink* in each box to make words.

 Cover each word and write it from memory.

p [ ] _____   s [ ] _____

shr [ ] _____   th [ ] _____

  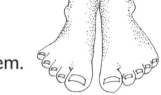

Now use these words to finish the poem.
Decorate it and give it a title.

Write each word carefully.

pink   shrink

sink   think

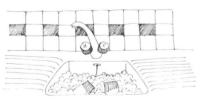

Now practise your handwriting.

I think they'll shrink in the sink.

I've a pair of _____ socks

I've washed in the _____.

The colour has run,

And I _____

That they'll _____.

Name . . . .

Trace over and then write the letter pattern.

int   int   int   int

Write each word carefully.

print

sprint

pint

Now practise your handwriting.

She intended to be a sprinter.

Write the letter pattern **int** in each box to make words.

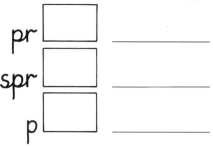 Cover each word and write it from memory.

pr [   ] _____

spr [   ] _____

p [   ] _____

Now finish the patterns.

print		printer	
	sprints		sprinter

Now finish the slogan.

Drink a ____ of ____ a day.

Name . . . .

Trace over and then write the letter pattern.

ite   *ite*   *ite*   *ite*

Write each word carefully.

excited

invite

invited

quite

unite

opposite

Now practise your handwriting.

The white house was opposite.

Write the letter pattern *ite* in each box to make words.

Cover each word and write it from memory.

exc [ ] d _____

inv [ ] _____

inv [ ] d _____

qu [ ] _____

un [ ] _____

oppos [ ] _____

Now use *ite* words to finish the poem.

I was really so _____

When I knew I was _____

To see my team _____ to play

Their final match on Saturday.

All in their blue and _____

Together they put up a fight,

But all in vain.

What a shame!

Name . . . .

Trace over and then write the letter pattern.

ive   ive   ive   ive

Write each word carefully.

alive   given   forgive

deliver   native

motive   expensive

Now practise your handwriting.

She delivers expensive presents.

Write the letter pattern ive in each box to make words.

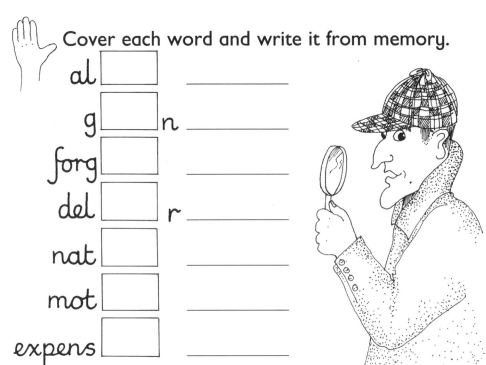

Cover each word and write it from memory.

al ☐ _____

g ☐ n _____

forg ☐ _____

del ☐ r _____

nat ☐ _____

mot ☐ _____

expens ☐ _____

Now use some of these words to finish the sentences.

1. The detective said the suspect had a _____.

2. Is it _____ to have the goods _____?

3. Please _____ my mistake.

© LDA A Hand for Spelling 4a

Name . . . .

Trace over and then write the word.

low *low* *low* *low*

Write each word carefully.

below   lower

pillow   slowly

flower

Now practise your handwriting.

The pillow fell below the bed.

Write the word **low** in each box to make words.

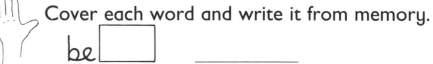

Cover each word and write it from memory.

be [ ] _____

[ ] er _____

pil [ ] _____

s [ ] ly _____

f [ ] er _____

Now finish the patterns.

glad	
	slowly
careful	
	smoothly

	juicy
flower	
	bumpy

Name . . . .

Trace over and then write the word.

man   man   man   man

Write each word carefully.

manage

manager

manner

fisherman

human

woman

Now practise your handwriting.

The fisherman managed a catch.

Write the word man in each box to make words.

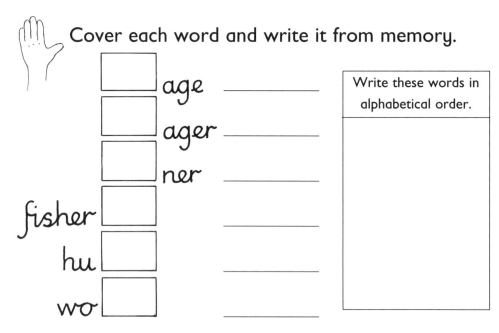

Cover each word and write it from memory.

☐ age _____

☐ ager _____

☐ ner _____

fisher ☐ _____

hu ☐ _____

wo ☐ _____

Write these words in
alphabetical order.

Now find the small words in the following word.

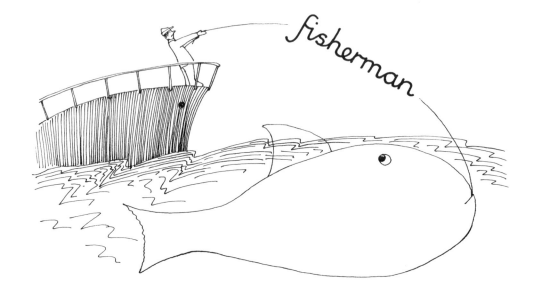

fisherman

Name . . . .

Trace over and then write the letter pattern.

med   med   med   med

Write each word carefully.

medical

medicine

mediate

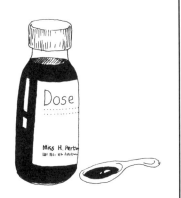

Now practise your handwriting.

She took her medicine.

Write the letter pattern **med** in each box to make words.

Cover each word and write it from memory.

☐ical _____   ☐iate _____

☐icine _____

Crossword

		1			2	3			
									4
5				6					
							7	8	
		9	10				11		
12						13			
		14				15			
		16							

Across
1. To act as peacemaker.
5. To do with illness.
7. Old word for father.
9. Last letters in 'duck'.
11. Large.
12. Swallow.
13. Small two letter word.
14. A refusal.
15. A small insect.
16. A female sheep.

Down
1. We take it when ill.
2. Everyone.
3. A large animal.
4. What you earn.
5. A mess.
6. an + d = _____ .
8. A female relative.
10. To understand.

83

Name . . . .

Trace over and then write the word.

met   met   met   met

Write each word carefully.

metal   metallic

metre   method

Now practise your handwriting.

I bought a metre of metal.

Write the word met in each box to make words.

Cover each word and write it from memory.

☐ al _____

☐ allic _____

☐ re _____

☐ hod _____

Now write the matching pairs of words.

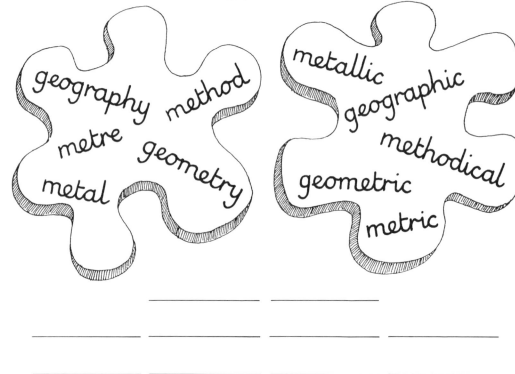

geography   method
metre   geometry
metal

metallic   geographic
methodical
geometric
metric

_____ _____ _____ _____

_____ _____ _____ _____

© LDA A Hand for Spelling 4a

Name . . . .

Trace over and then write the letter pattern.

mon   mon   mon   mon

Write each word carefully.

monster   money

monkey   month

pocket money!

Now practise your handwriting.

How much money this month?

Write the letter pattern mon in each box to make words.

Cover each word and write it from memory.

☐ ster _____

☐ ey _____

☐ key _____

☐ th _____

Write these words in alphabetical order.

Now finish the pattern.

Singular	Plural
monster	
	months
monkey	

Finish the puzzles with mon words.

1. a day of the week

2. a precious stone

☐

☐

Name . . . .

Trace over and then write the letter pattern.

mot   *mot*   *mot*   *mot*

Write each word carefully.

motion   motive

motor   moth

mothers

Now practise your handwriting.

a moth in motion

Write the letter pattern **mot** in each box to make words.

Cover each word and write it from memory.

☐ ion _____
☐ ive _____
☐ or _____
☐ h _____
☐ hers _____

Write these words in alphabetical order.

Now rewrite the phrases using a word with an apostrophe and 's' instead of the underlined word.

The day belonging to <u>mother</u>.

_____

The wings belonging to the <u>moth</u>.

_____

The switch belonging to the <u>motor</u>.

_____

Name . . . .

Trace over and then write the letter pattern.

ner   *ner*   *ner*   *ner*

Write each word carefully.

corner   energy

nervous   partner

Now practise your handwriting.

My brother was nervous.

Write the letter pattern *ner* in each box to make words.

 Cover each word and write it from memory.

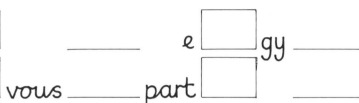

cor ☐ _____   e ☐ gy _____

☐ vous _____ part ☐ _____

Words are often linked with other words in meaning. Now use these words to link each group.

strength, power, life, =

afraid, excited, butterflies in your stomach =

friend, one of a pair =

point where two lines meet, part of a room =

Name . . . .

Trace over and then write the word.

oar   *oar*   *oar*   *oar*

Write each word carefully.

aboard   boar

board   cardboard

cupboard

Now practise your handwriting.

The boar lay on the boards.

Write the word *oar* in each box to make words.

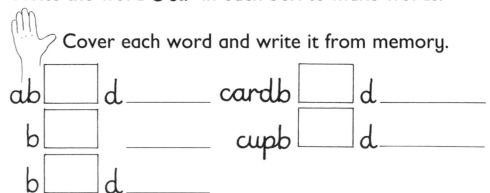

Cover each word and write it from memory.

ab ☐ d _____   cardb ☐ d _____

b ☐ _____   cupb ☐ d _____

b ☐ d _____

A **compound** word is a word made up of two other words. Now use the following words to make compound words. Some words can be used more than once.

card   birth   over

tea

cup   board   day

© LDA A Hand for Spelling 4a

Name . . . .

Trace over and then write the letter pattern.

oas   oas   oas   oas

Write the letter pattern **oas** in each box to make words.

Cover each word and write it from memory.

c ⬜ t _____   t ⬜ t _____

r ⬜ t _____   ⬜ is _____

Now write in meanings for the dictionary words.

Write each word carefully.

coast   roast

toast

oasis

Now practise your handwriting.

toast by a roasting fire

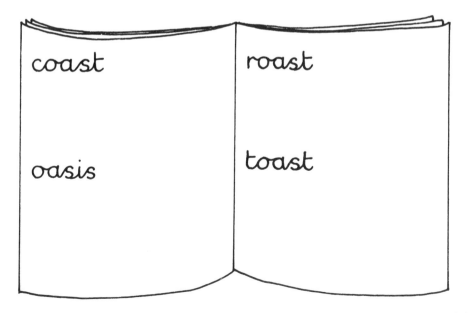

coast   roast

oasis   toast

Name . . . .

Trace over and then write the letter pattern.

 oat   oat   oat   oat

Write each word carefully.

boat   coat

float   goat

throat

Now practise your handwriting.

The boat is afloat.

Write the letter pattern oat in each box to make words.

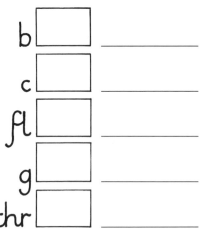 Cover each word and write it from memory.

b ☐ _____
c ☐ _____
fl ☐ _____
g ☐ _____
thr ☐ _____

Match the jigsaw pieces and write out the pairs of words.

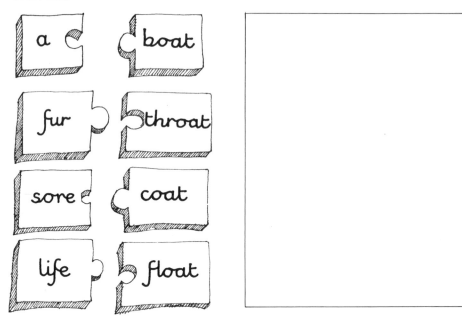

© LDA A Hand for Spelling 4a